The doe nestles into the nesting box. It is time for her kindling. Soon, she will have a new litter of babies.

The rabbit hutch is warm and cozy. The doe hops into her nesting box. **Sniff, sniff, sniff.** Everything smells safe.

An adult female rabbit is called a doe.

visit us at www.abdopublishing.com

Published by Magic Wagon, a division of the ABDO Group, 8000 West 78th Street, Edina, Minnesota 55439. Copyright © 2010 by Abdo Consulting Group, Inc. International copyrights reserved in all countries. All rights reserved. No part of this book may be reproduced in any form without written permission from the publisher.

Looking Glass Library™ is a trademark and logo of Magic Wagon.

Printed in the United States.

 Manufactured with paper containing at least 10% post-consumer waste

Text by Patricia M. Stockland
Illustrations by Todd Ouren
Edited by Amy Van Zee
Interior layout and design by Becky Daum
Cover design by Becky Daum

Library of Congress Cataloging-in-Publication Data
Stockland, Patricia M.
 In the rabbit hutch / by Patricia M. Stockland ; illustrated by Todd Ouren.
     p. cm. — (Barnyard buddies)
 Includes index.
 ISBN 978-1-60270-645-3
 1. Rabbits—Juvenile literature. I. Ouren, Todd, ill. II. Title.
SF453.2.S82 2010
636.932'2—dc22
                                        2009007490

In the Rabbit Hutch

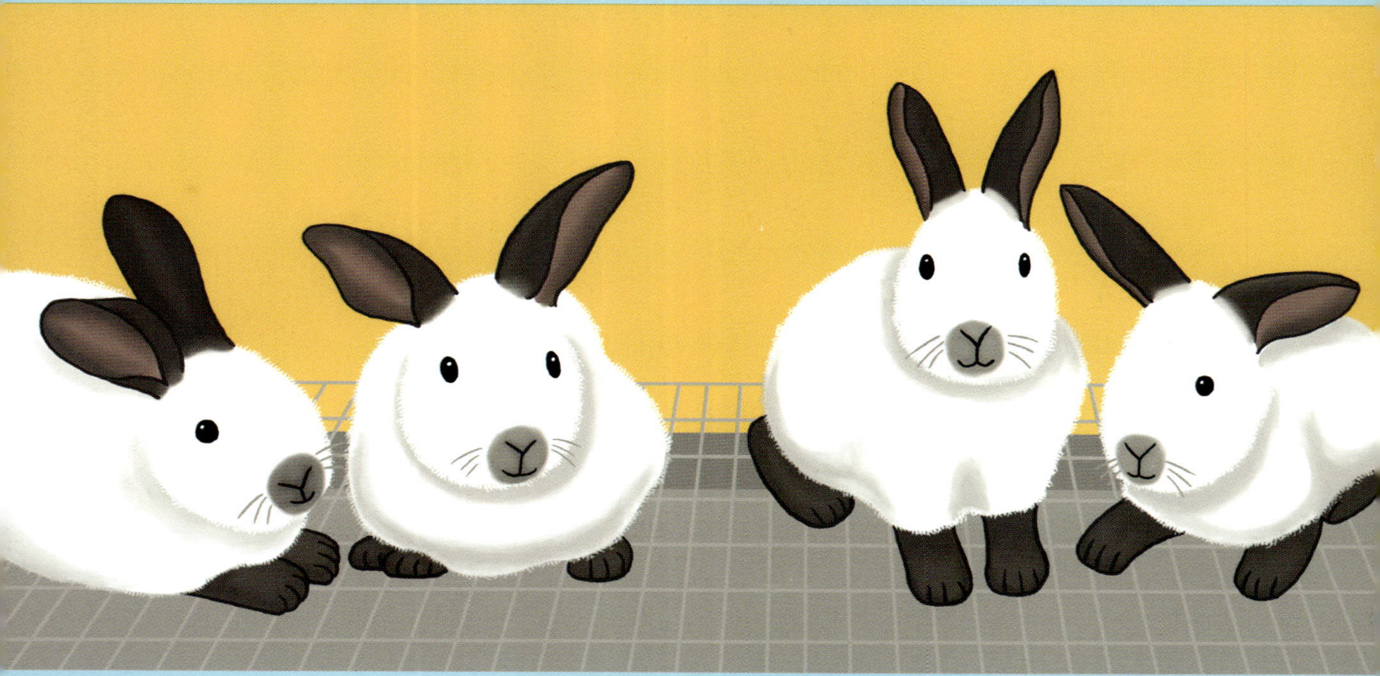

by Patricia M. Stockland
illustrated by Todd Ouren

Special thanks to content consultant:
James S. Cullor, DVM, PhD

Kindling is when a doe gives birth.

The new babies are very tiny. They need the doe's care to stay safe, warm, and fed. The doe uses straw and her fur to keep the babies warm.

Rabbits are born without fur.

The growing babies are very hungry. The baby rabbits drink milk from their mother.

The doe stays upright and watchful while she nurses her litter.

When the rabbits are about three weeks old, the farmer takes away their nesting box. The rabbits have grown enough fur to stay warm and safe without it.

A nesting box is a safe place inside a hutch.
The hutch is a bigger house for the rabbits.

The young rabbits explore their hutch. They play and hop. They also learn to eat solid foods. The farmer brings fresh hay every day.

Rabbits like to eat alfalfa hay. They also eat oats, grasses, and some vegetables.

When the rabbits are six weeks old, the farmer weans them from the doe. They are big enough to live on their own.

Weaning is when a rabbit is separated from its mother.

Some rabbits are big enough to go to market. Other rabbits stay on the farm.

Farmers raise rabbits for meat, fur, showing, and as pets.

The farmer helps the remaining rabbits grow to be healthy does and bucks. The best rabbits go to the county fair to be shown.

At a fair or a show, rabbits are judged on health, fur, and personality.

The rabbits return to the farm. Soon, they will have litters of their own. **Sniff, sniff, sniff.** It is good to smell home.

Rabbit Diagram

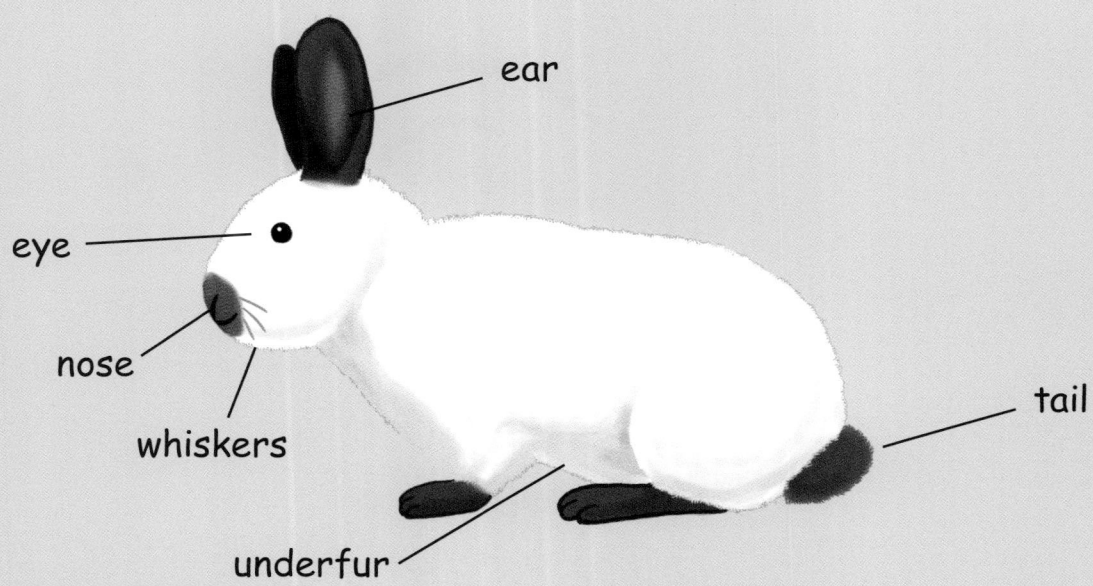

Glossary

buck—an adult male rabbit.
hutch—the shelter in which rabbits are raised and live.
litter—a group of babies born to a doe.
market—where animals are bought and sold.
nesting box—a box that is put inside a hutch and filled with hay. A nesting box is a safe place for a rabbit to give birth.
personality—an animal's qualities and traits.

Fun Facts

 There are many different kinds of rabbits. Cottontail rabbits and European rabbits are the most common types of rabbits in the wild.

 Rabbits have scent glands in their chins. A scent gland leaves a smell. A rabbit will rub its chin on something. That lets other rabbits know the object is taken.

 A doe usually has four to ten babies at a time. Some litters might have more than ten babies.

 Rabbits are very protective of their territory. Sometimes a rabbit will leave a trail of droppings to mark an area. This tells other rabbits that the area already belongs to another rabbit!

 When a rabbit is angry, it will grunt. Rabbits can also make shrieking sounds. They purr when they're happy.

 A pet rabbit might beg for a treat, just like a dog!

 Rabbits use their whiskers to sense how large an area is and to feel their surroundings in the dark. This is similar to how a cat uses its whiskers.

Index

buck 18
doe 3, 4, 5, 6, 8, 9, 14, 18
fairs 18, 19
farmer 10, 12, 14, 17, 18
food 8, 12, 13
fur 6, 7, 10, 17, 19
hutch 3, 11, 12
kindling 4, 5
litter 4, 9, 20
market 16
nesting box 3, 4, 10, 11
wean 14, 15